Learn piano in

collection

Learn piano *KEYS*
in 10 minutes!

#1

smart funnies

j.steele · all ages

easy

visual

Learn piano *NOTES*
in 10 minutes!

#2

smart funnies

j.steele · all ages

easy

visual

Learn piano *SYMBOLS*
in 10 minutes!

#3

smart funnies

j.steele · all ages

easy

visual

j.steele

all ages

easy

visual

Series

best completed **in order**

After **all 3** lessons,

you'll know Piano BASICS!

Learn piano *KEYS*

in 10 minutes!

#1

**Published by
Jolieco®LLC
Danville, CA**

j.steele

easy

visual

to Joe, Jasmine & Jade
who inspired this series

sometimes . . .

less
is
MORE

contents

How to **learn piano KEYS**

in 10 minutes . . .

1. keep it simple

2. Pictures are worth a thousand words!

> **Visual Learning**
> a proven method
>
> **promotes quick understanding**

✓ no piano required for this lesson.

black keys REPEAT
sets of 2's
and 3's

2
black

3
black

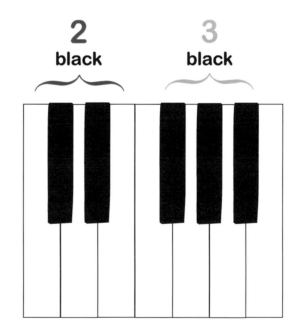

white keys

black keys help us find

white keys

like landmarks . . .

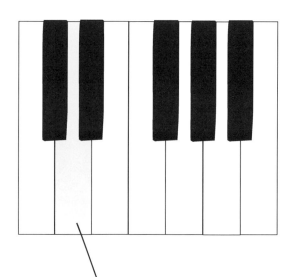

I'm the white key
between
2 black keys!

white keys

imagine . . .

white keys as
ANIMALS and **KIDS**

2 or 3
black keys
help us
remember

WHICH is WHICH

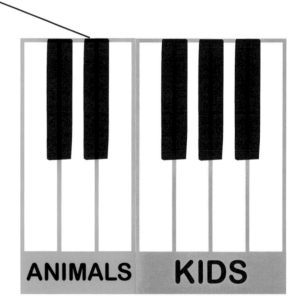

ANIMALS   **KIDS**

tip alert!

my friend calls
2 black keys
"a Doghouse"

. . . see **"Dog"**
inside his house
on the next page

white keys

white keys
below **2 black** keys

"ANIMALS"

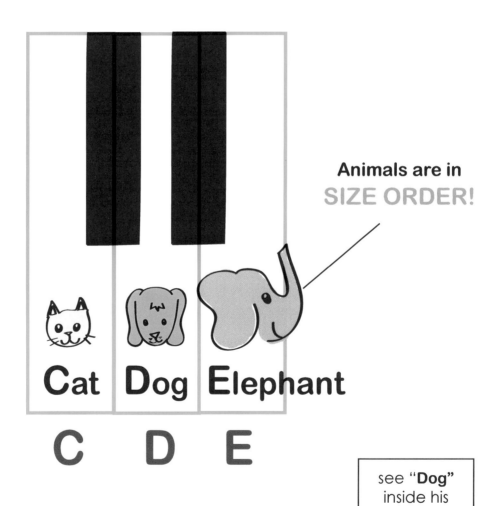

Animals are in
SIZE ORDER!

Cat **Dog** **Elephant**

C **D** **E**

see **"Dog"**
inside his
Doghouse?

white keys

white keys
below **3 black** keys

"KIDS"

Funny **Girls** **And** **Boys**

F G A B

white keys

ANIMALS + KIDS

black keys
are your clues (including the "Doghouse")...

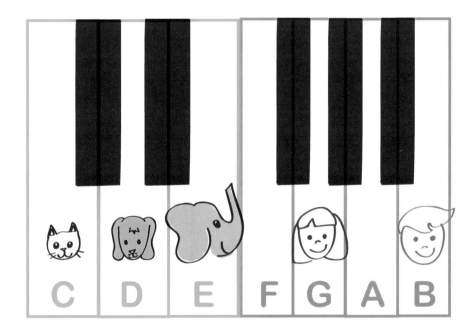

this pattern REPEATS up & down the keyboard!

14

white keys

examples

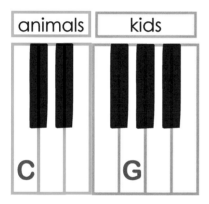

animals — C

kids — G

remember,
black keys
are your clues!

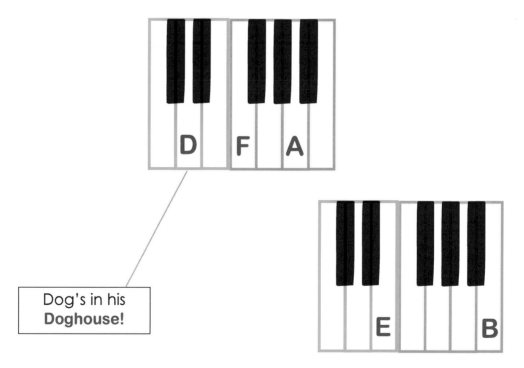

D   F   A

Dog's in his
Doghouse!

E   B

white keys

now you know

the

white keys!

go ahead,

test yourself on the next page . . .

gopher's CHALLENGE *white keys*

. . . can you name these *white keys*?

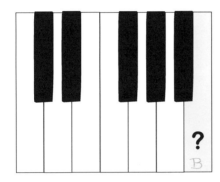

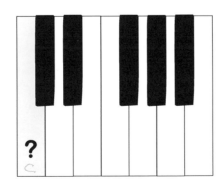

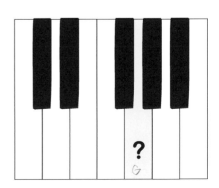

answers next page . . .

gopher's CHALLENGE answers

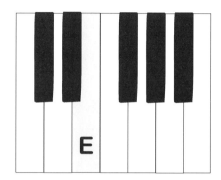

E

how did you do?

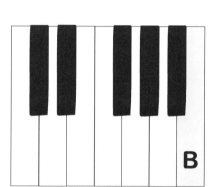

B

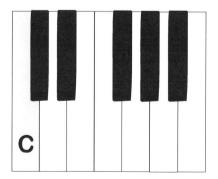

C

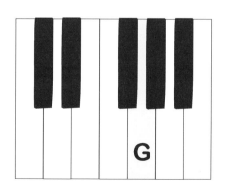

G

white keys

important KEY to know!

"Middle C"

C closest to the
middle of the keyboard

↓

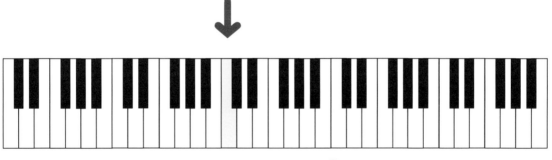

white keys

black keys
are called

"Sharps" and "Flats"

SECRET of the black keys?

remember this **ARROW** point . . .

"flat"   "sharp"

notice "flat" side
of arrow is on LEFT

see how the
**"sharp" tip
points RIGHT?**

from any *white key* ☺

closest key **RIGHT** = "sharp"

LEFT = "flat" ♭

next closest key
is usually
(but not always)
a BLACK KEY!

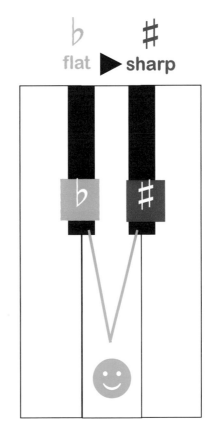

black keys

example

from any **D**-key

closest key RIGHT = "**D**-sharp"

LEFT = "**D**-flat"

D♯ D♭
are both
BLACK KEYS

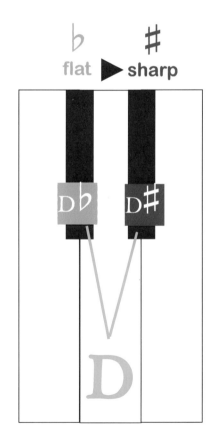

flat ▶ sharp

black keys

black keys
can be

BOTH sharp and flat

see how
**I'm BOTH
Sharp & Flat?**

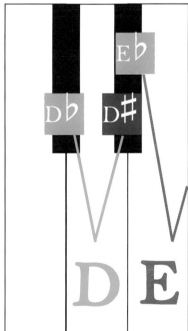

♭   ♯
flat ▶ sharp

If next closest key is *white,*

sharp or flat
can be *white keys!*

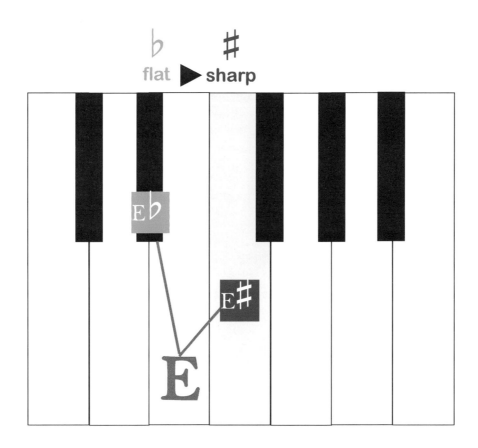

flat ▶ sharp

black keys

examples

flat ▶ sharp

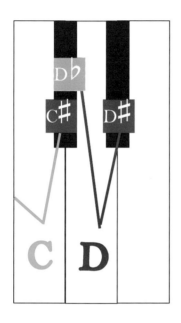

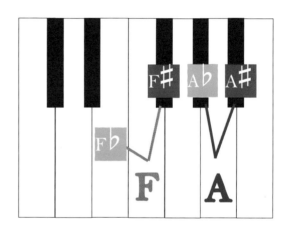

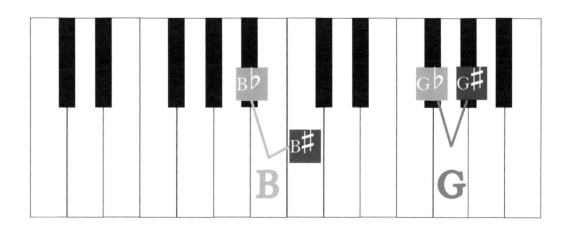

black keys

you've learned

the

black keys!

"you're awesome!"

JUDGE

test yourself on the next page . . .

gopher's CHALLENGE black keys

can you name these **black keys?**

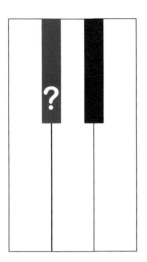 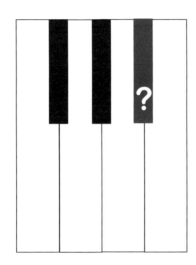 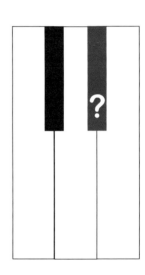

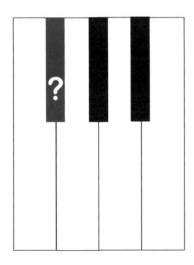

hint:
more than
one answer
for each key!

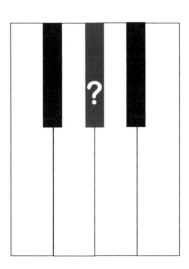

27

answers next page . . .

gopher's CHALLENGE

answers

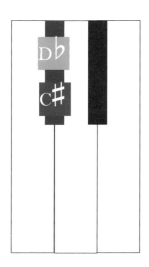

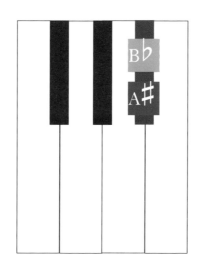

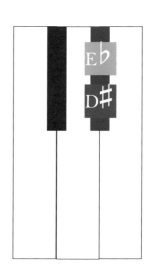

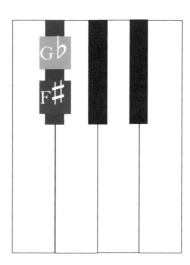

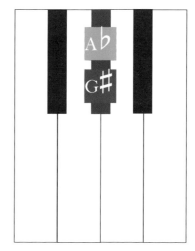

flat ▶ sharp

black keys

. . . that completes

white keys
&
black keys!

Has it been 10 minutes yet?

traffic around Middle C

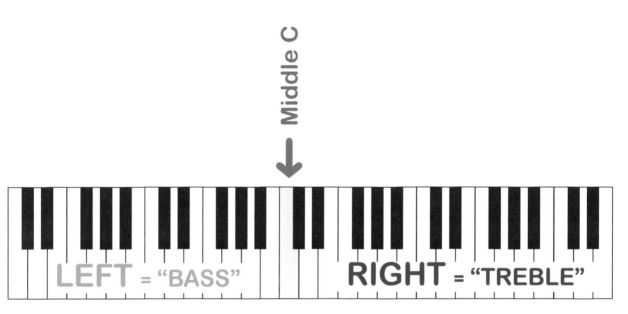

Middle C

LEFT = "BASS"

RIGHT = "TREBLE"

lower, down, below
middle C

higher, up, above
middle C

"TREBLE" and "BASS" (say "base")
become very important
in 10-minute book #3 on Symbols

keyboard terms

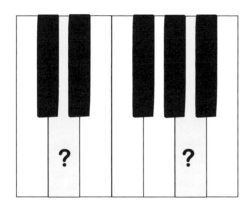

can you name
these keys?

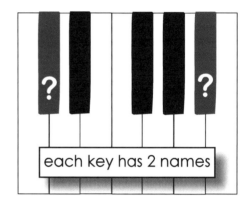

each key has 2 names

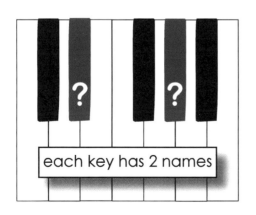

each key has 2 names

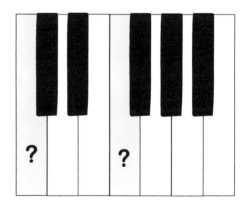

good luck!

answers next page . . .

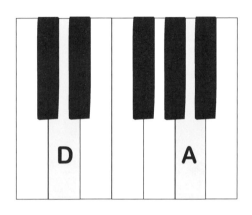

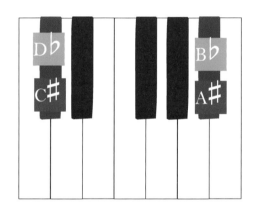

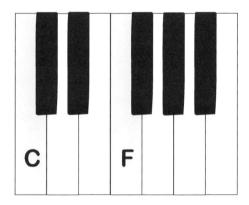

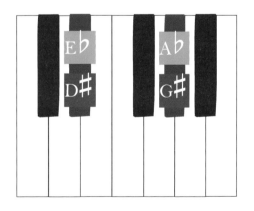

how did you do?

"You Did It!"

Zzzz

Series

best completed **in order**

10-minute Lesson #1   KEYS

10-minute Lesson #2   NOTES

10-minute Lesson #3   SYMBOLS

After **all 3** lessons,
you'll know Piano BASICS!

Learn piano *NOTES*

in 10 minutes!

#2

easy

visual

Published by
Jolieco®LLC
Danville, CA

j.steele

sometimes . . .

less
is
MORE

author's preface

contents

DO
CURVE FINGERS GENTLY

DON'T
play with fingers "straight out"

The SECRET

if you can remember
2 simple "Funnies"

. . . you can read NOTES!

images help your memory

funny #1

Green Beans

"Green Beans Do Fly

At Ed

Green Beans Do Fly"

memory tip:
**remember
IMAGES!**

**this is
Ed**

1. say WORDS

2. study IMAGE

3. repeat

try to
"burn" this funny
into memory!

can you

REPEAT "Green Beans"

one more time?
without peeking

gopher's CHALLENGE
"Green Beans"

1. what food appears?

2. what does it "Do"?

3. where does it "Do" this?

4. how often is "Green" repeated?

answers next page . . .

1. **what food appears?**

    Green beans

2. **what does it "Do"?**

    "Do" fly

3. **where does it "Do" this?**

    At Ed!

4. **how often is "Green" repeated?**

    twice!!

Don't forget about **"Ed"**

funny #2

ACE

"ACE - Got - FACE"

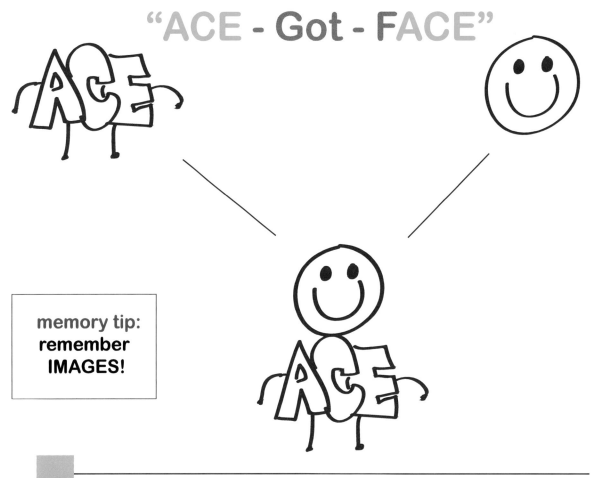

memory tip:
remember
IMAGES!

1. say WORDS

2. study IMAGE

3. repeat

can you
"burn" this funny
into memory
too?

can you

REPEAT "ACE"

one more time?
without peeking

1. what is the character's name?

2. what did he "Get"?

3. which 2 words rhyme?

4. what "G" word is in the middle?

1. **what is the character's name?**

    Ace

2. **what did he "Get"?**

    Face

3. **which 2 words rhyme?**

    Ace & Face

4. **what "G" word is in the middle?**

    Got!

    (don't forget this "G" word, ok?)

piano NOTES appear on
LINES & SPACES

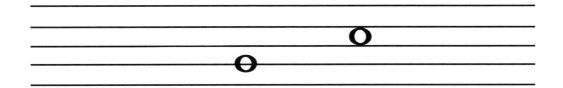

**5 lines + 4 spaces
are called a "STAFF"**

each NOTE
= a SOUND!

the staff

2 Staffs
connected

create a
"GRAND STAFF"

TREBLE

BASS (say "base")

tip: "base" can also mean "bottom"

TREBLE is "higher" than **BASS!**

the staff

let's add the
GRAND STAFF

to
our
Funnies!

if you remember
BOTH Funnies,
you can read
NOTES

"Green Beans"

are notes on **LINES!**

TREBLE

Fly
Do
Beans
Green
Ed

BASS

At
Fly
Do
Beans
Green

start here!

the staff

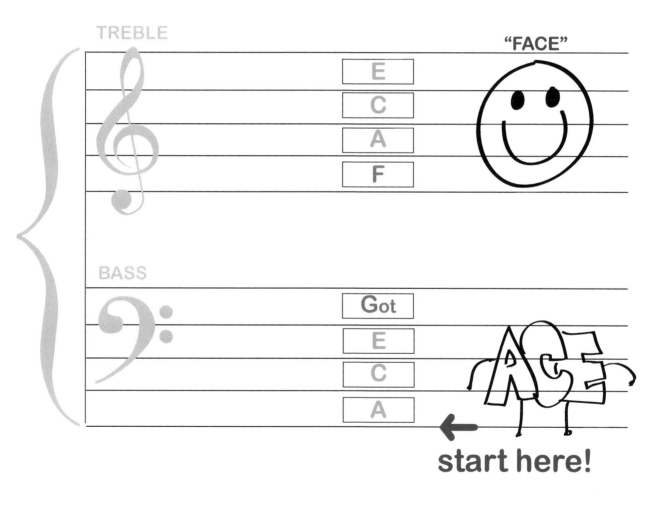

"ACE"

are notes in SPACES!

TREBLE

"FACE"

| E |
| C |
| A |
| F |

BASS

| Got |
| E |
| C |
| A |

start here!

easy memory tips!

"Green Beans"

are straight like **LINES**

"ACE"

rhymes with **SPACE**

Grand Staff

both funnies!

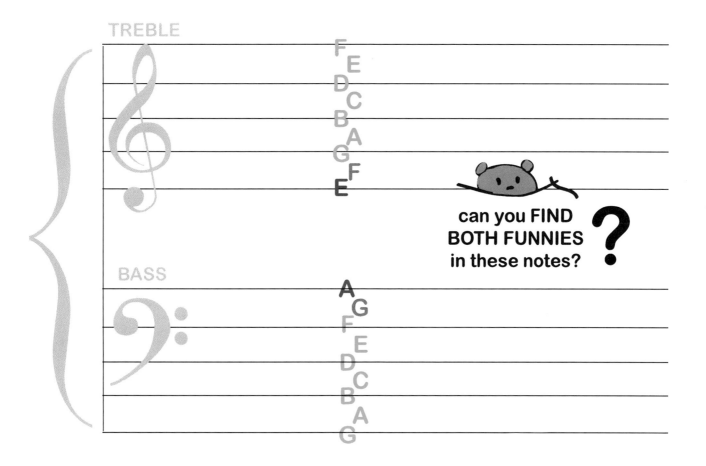

TREBLE

F
E
D
C
B
A
G
F
E

can you FIND
BOTH FUNNIES
in these notes?

BASS

A
G
F
E
D
C
B
A
G

know this **Note!**

"Middle C"

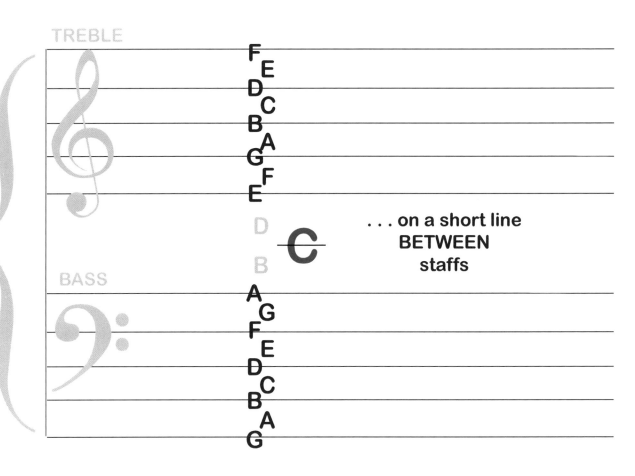

. . . on a short line
BETWEEN
staffs

alphabet repeats A to G

. . . including both spaces
above & below Middle C

how does it feel?

you can
read NOTES!

"so proud of you!"

Has it been 10 minutes yet?

"sight-read" Notes

SAME line/space = SAME key

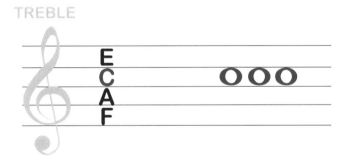

 press **C** key
3 times!

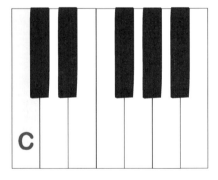

tips

what's moved?

in these
Sharps & Flats

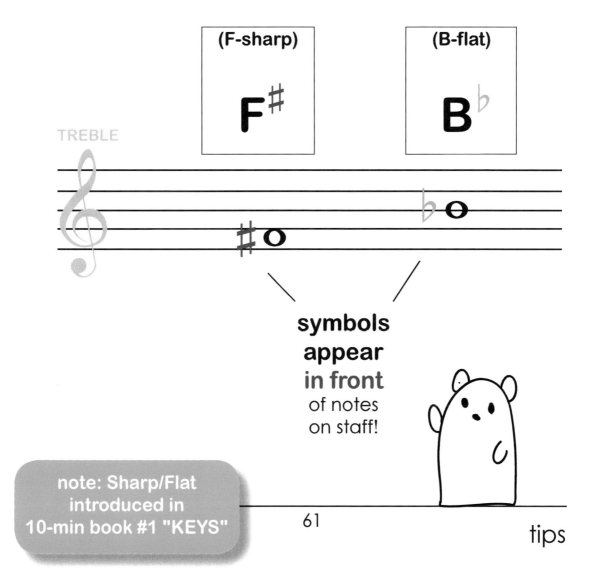

(F-sharp) — F#

(B-flat) — B♭

TREBLE

symbols
appear
in front
of notes
on staff!

note: Sharp/Flat
introduced in
10-min book #1 "KEYS"

61

tips

Naturally, dear gopher!

SHARP ♯
& FLAT ♭
<u>carry forward</u> for the same note

UNTIL . . .

"NATURAL" symbol

CANCELS previous Sharp/Flat
so you play the *white key*

tips

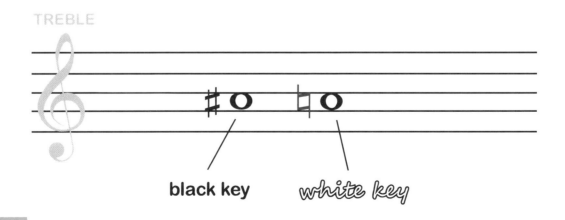

black key   *white key*

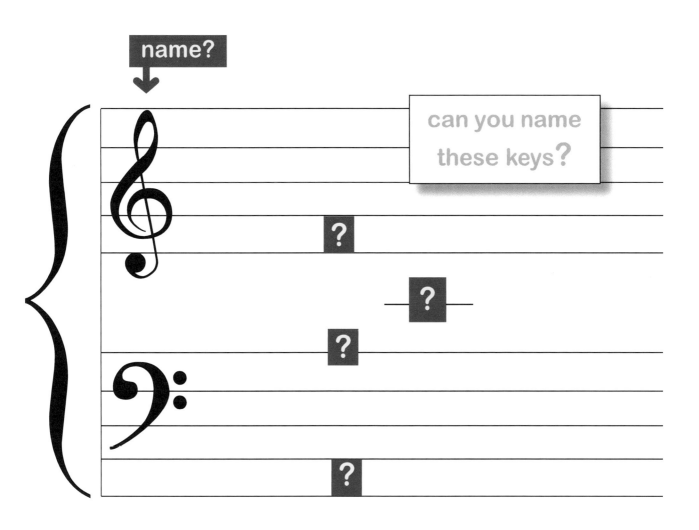

answers next page . . .

gopher's CHALLENGE

answers

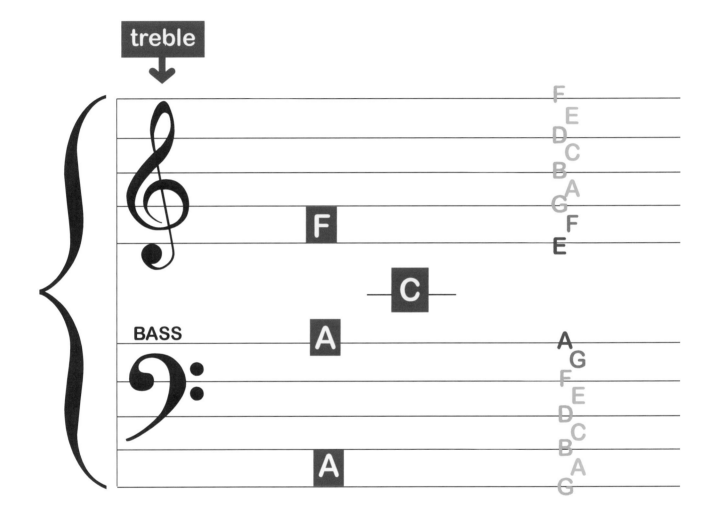

treble

BASS

you did it!

for extra credit:

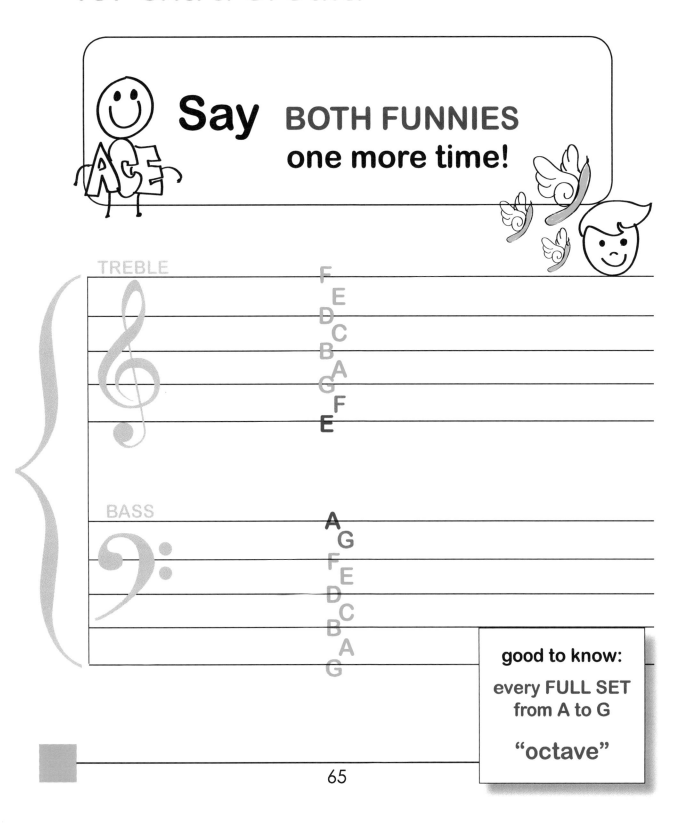

Series

best completed **in order**

10-minute Lesson #1 KEYS ✓

10-minute Lesson #2 NOTES ✓

10-minute Lesson #3 SYMBOLS

After **all 3** lessons,
you'll know Piano BASICS!

Learn piano *SYMBOLS*

in 10 minutes!

#3

easy

visual

Published by
Jolieco®LLC
Danville, CA

j.steele

sometimes . . .

less
is
MORE

author's preface

contents

OK,
this is the final
10-minute lesson.

You can do it!

TREBLE & BASS

(say "base")

TREBLE & BASS
"notes"

. . . tell you which **"keys"** to play!

follow me . . .
I'll show you
on the next page

treble & bass

TREBLE "keys"

RIGHT of middle C

middle C

"higher up"
the keyboard

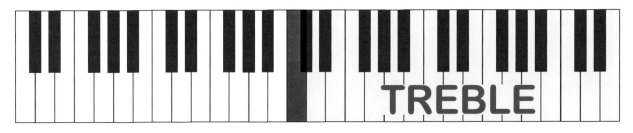

TREBLE

R

. . . often played
RIGHT-HANDED!

BASS "keys"

LEFT of middle C

"lower down"
the keyboard

middle C

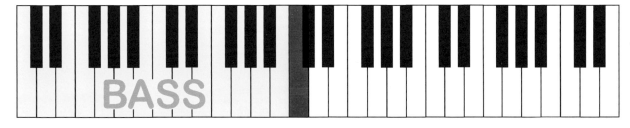

BASS

L

. . . often played
LEFT-HANDED!

treble & bass

TREBLE "notes"

ABOVE middle C
higher sounds!

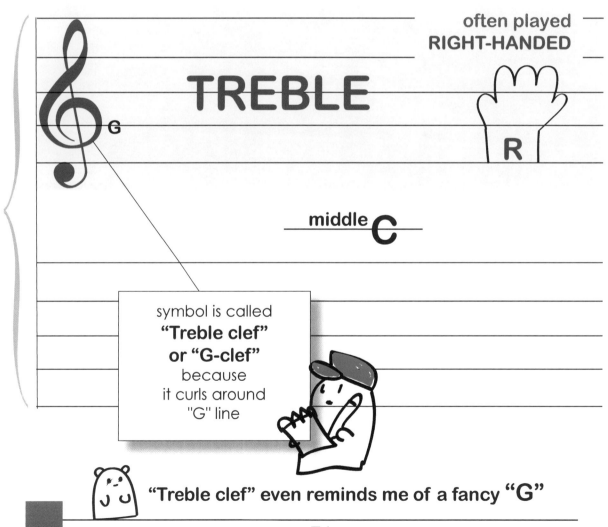

TREBLE

often played
RIGHT-HANDED

R

G

middle **C**

symbol is called
**"Treble clef"
or "G-clef"**
because
it curls around
"G" line

"Treble clef" even reminds me of a fancy **"G"**

BASS "notes"

BELOW middle C
...lower **sounds**

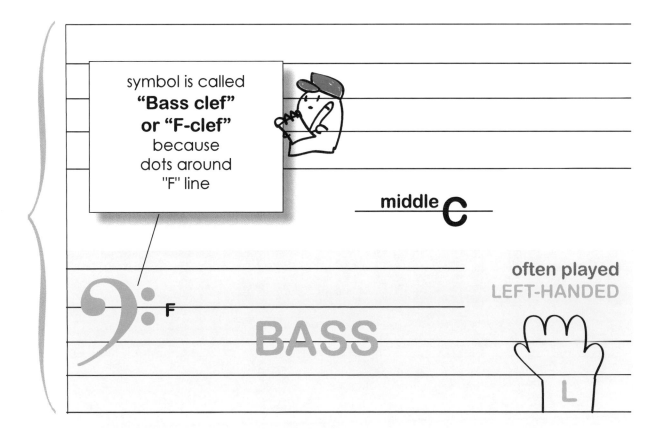

symbol is called **"Bass clef" or "F-clef"** because dots around "F" line

middle **C**

F

BASS

often played LEFT-HANDED

L

 2 dots on "Bass clef" remind me of 2 lines on **"F"**

TREBLE + BASS

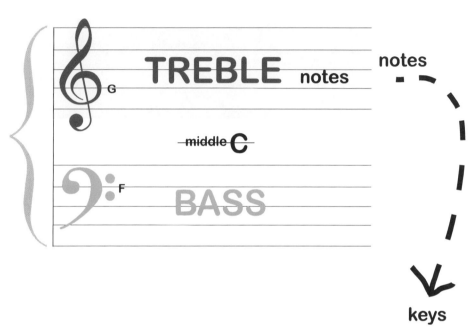

TREBLE notes

middle C

BASS

notes

keys

"lower"

"higher"

BASS C TREBLE keys!

L R

what if BOTH staffs TREBLE?

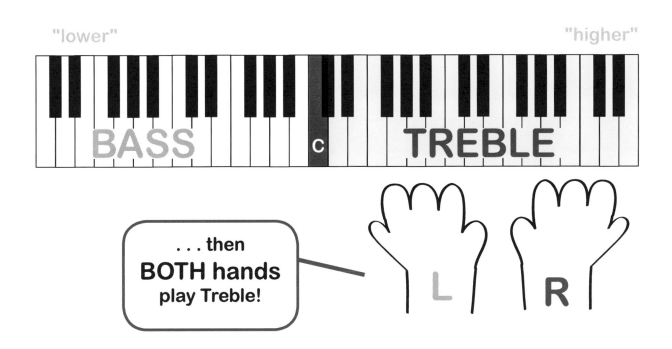

piano NOTES
have different
Shapes

these Shapes tell us
how long to play a key!

each Shape
has a
"COUNT"

counts

"COUNTS" are easy!

"count" this **silently** in your head

"1...2...3...4"

↓

4 counts

got it!

"half" of 4 counts =
2 counts
"1...2"

counts

meet a **4** COUNT note!

o

also called a
"whole" note

to play a "whole" note,
hold the piano key down
while counting 1...2...3...4
(a very long note)

counts

SHAPES & "COUNTS"

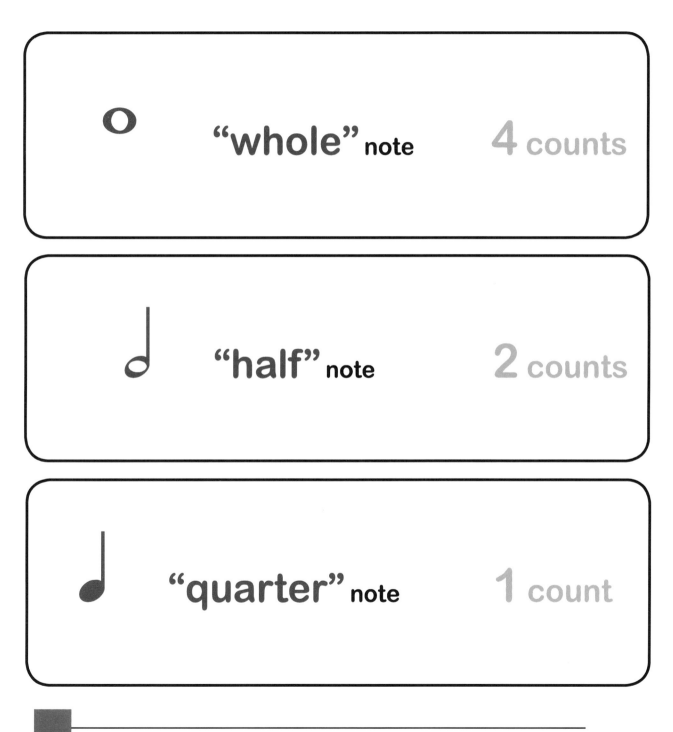

O "**whole**"**note**   **4** counts

"**half**"**note**   **2** counts

"**quarter**"**note**   **1** count

counts

Gopher's easy memory tips!

"whole" **4** counts

ho**llow** like a **balloon** rising **slowly** for 4 counts . . .

"half" **2** counts

imagine a whole note **cut in half** by the "stem"

"quarter" **1** count

solid like a **stone** falling quickly in 1 count!

---

counts

"dotted half"   3 counts

- **side dot** adds 1 extra count to "half" notes

"eighth" note   ½ count

racing flag speed = **1 quick tap** on keyboard

"eighth" notes **connected!**

2 quick taps

(½ count each)

tip: "stems" on notes can point up or down

1 count
SILENCE!

**called a
"Quarter REST"**

counts

2 or 4 counts

SILENCE!

2 counts	4 counts
SILENCE	**SILENCE**
"Half REST"	"Whole REST"

think of "Whole RESTS" as
Clouds rising high
. . . very, very, very, very SILENTLY

play 1 note
even LONGER

notes on **SAME line/space**
can be **"TIED"** together
to **ADD** their counts

example above:

2 counts + 3 counts

= hold this **SAME NOTE**
longer for **5 counts!**

86

counts

play 2 (or more) notes TOGETHER

press all 3 keys at the SAME TIME!

this is called a

"CHORD"

87

. . . divide music into EQUAL COUNTS
or "measures"

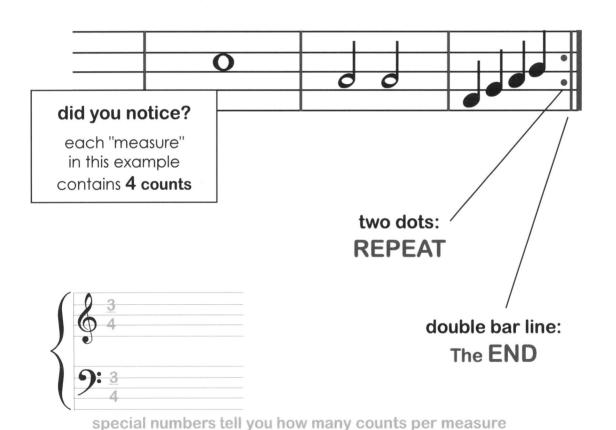

did you notice?

each "measure"
in this example
contains **4 counts**

two dots:
REPEAT

double bar line:
The END

special numbers tell you how many counts per measure
(look at the "top" number, so 3 counts per measure here)

counts

"staccato" jumping dots!

fingers
JUMP QUICKLY,
popping like
popcorn!

think of
jumping
beans

"legato"   smooth

a
curve
over/under
a group of notes

**play notes
rolling
SMOOTHLY,
fingers
almost gliding!**

opposite of staccato

"rit."

. . . slow down, slowly

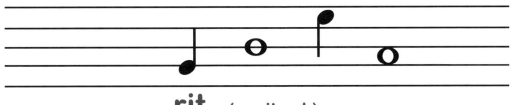

rit. (or ritard.)

gradually
SLOW DOWN
when
playing
these notes

(full word is "ritardando")

"accent" LOUDLY!

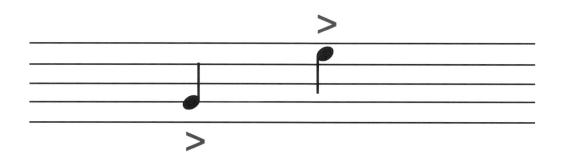

play these notes

 LOUDER

than others!

HOW LOUD to play a song?

look for these **symbols**

"*p*"
(piano)
= SOFT
p for peep?

"*mp*"
(mezzo piano)
= medium SOFT
m for medium?

"*mf*"
(mezzo forte)
= medium LOUD

"*f*"
(forte)
= LOUD!
f for forceful?

crescendo = gradually LOUDER

decrescendo
(or diminuendo)
= gradually SOFTER

Has it been 10 minutes yet?

gopher's CHALLENGE

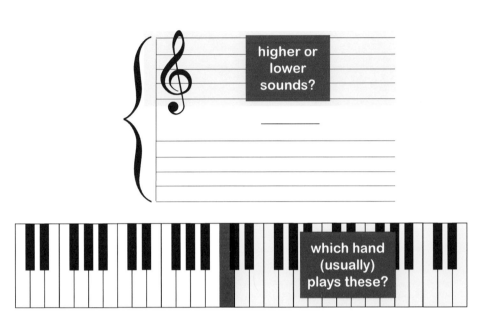

higher or lower sounds?

_____

which hand (usually) plays these?

how many COUNTS?	play LOUD or SOFT?	what SOUND do these make?
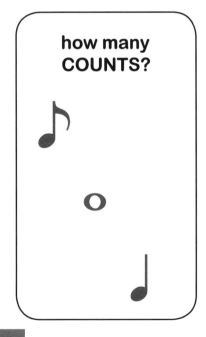	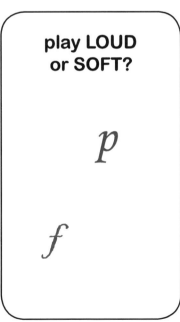	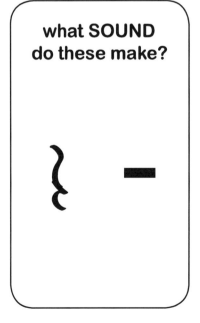

answers next page . . .

HIGHER sounds

RIGHT hand (usually)

---

how many COUNTS?

♪ = ½ count

○ = 4 counts

♩ = 1 count

---

play LOUD or SOFT?

p = SOFT

f = LOUD

---

what SOUND do these make?

= NONE!
(counts of silence)

Sight-read!

memory tips from past lessons in Series

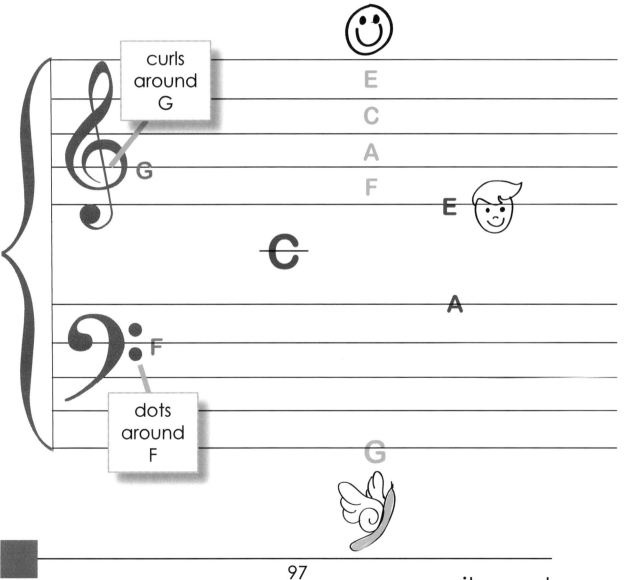

site-read

Series

best completed **in order**

10-minute Lesson #1   KEYS ✓

10-minute Lesson #2   NOTES ✓

10-minute Lesson #3   SYMBOLS ✓

Congratulations

. . . you know
Piano BASICS!

CPSIA information can be obtained
at www.ICGtesting.com
Printed in the USA
LVIW020418041212
309992LV00007B